AF570649

Antarctica

Sarah Fleming

Contents

Meet Bernard Stonehouse

Bernard has been going to Antarctica since 1946. He has mapped pieces of Antarctica and studied penguins and other wildlife there. Throughout the book Bernard gives personal reports about some of his experiences in Antarctica.

Where Is Antarctica?

Antarctica (say Ant–ARK–tih–kuh) is the **continent** at the South **Pole**.

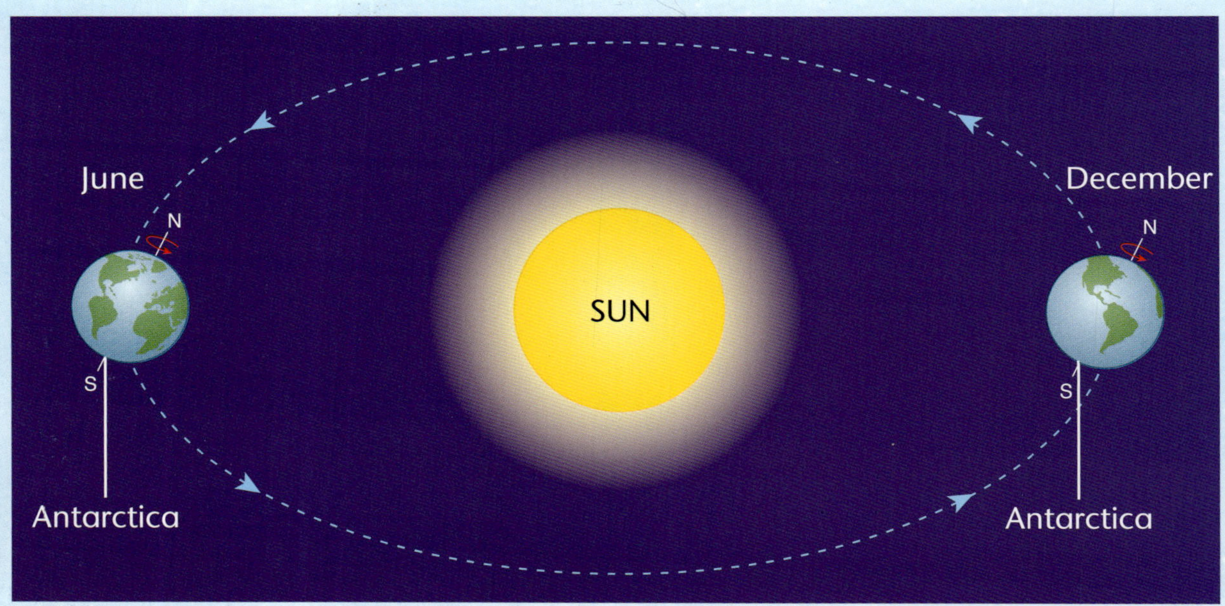

At the South Pole, it is light for half of the year and dark for the other half.

The ice at the North Pole just floats on the water, so it is not a continent. At the South Pole the ice covers land, so it is a continent.

DEFINITIONS

continent: one of the seven very large land areas in the world

pole: the farthest point south or north in the world. The earth turns around these imaginary poles.

Standing at 9,163 feet (2,793 m) above **sea level** (8,705 feet, or 2,653 m, of that is ice).

This pole marks the South Pole. It is stuck into the ice, but the ice covering the land is always moving slowly toward the sea. Every so often, the pole has to be put back in the right place.

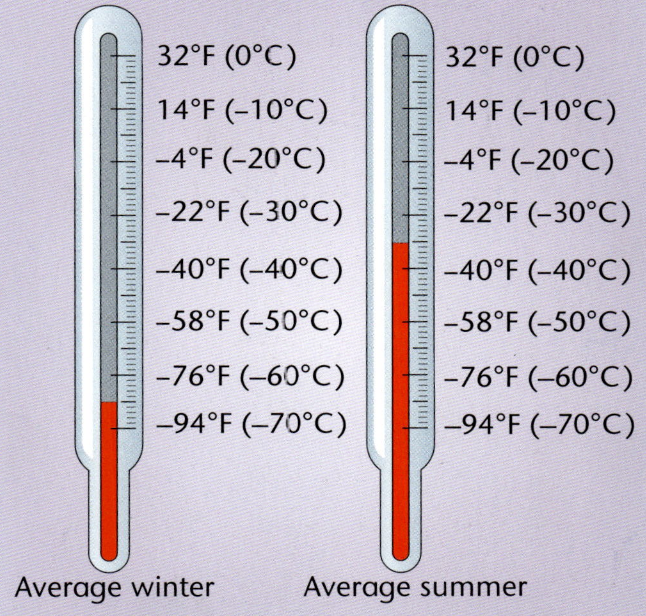

Average winter temperature –85°F (–65°C)

Average summer temperature –31°F (–35°C)

Getting There

Antarctica is difficult to get to. To get there by ship, you have to cross the southern ocean.

There is not much land around Antarctica, so high water and very strong winds build up.

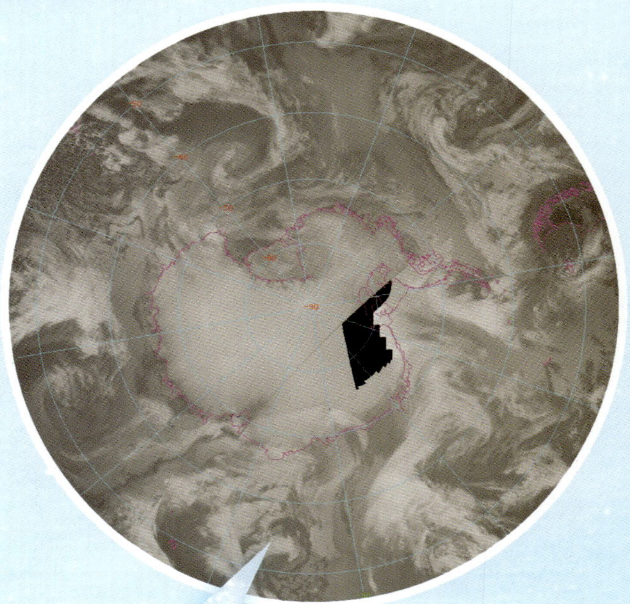

Huge storm winds and waves as big as a house are normal.

Icy seas all year long

You also have to get across icy seas. In the winter, half of the southern ocean freezes over completely, making Antarctica twice its real size. For eight months of the year, you cannot get to the Antarctic **mainland** by sea.

In the summer, some of the sea ice (**pack ice**) breaks up, and ships can get through. This pack ice is always moving with the sea. Ships can get squashed between **floes**.

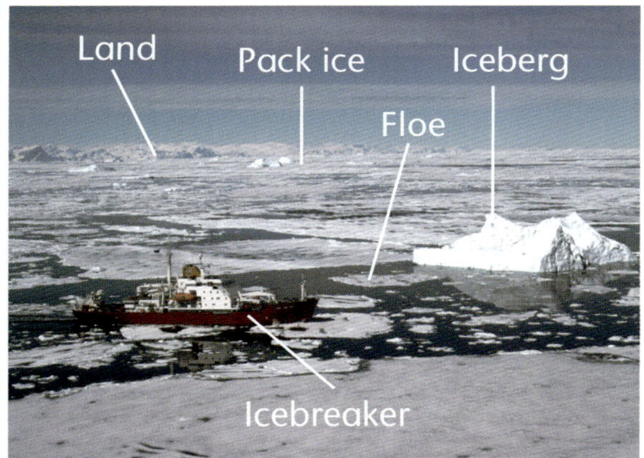

Summer

1915

British explorer Ernest Shackleton's ship got caught in the pack ice. It was pulled around by the currents, then crushed and broken by the ice. It sank.

DEFINITIONS

mainland: the main part of a continent or country. Antarctica has a large mainland with many smaller islands around it.

pack ice: ice that has formed a sheet on the ocean, and then is broken into blocks by the swell of the water. The blocks are called **floes** (say "flows"). Floes can be up to 20 feet (6 m) thick and 932 miles (1,500 km) across.

It's much easier to fly!

Exploration

As early as 1422, the Chinese may have mapped some of the Antarctic islands.

From Cook's Diary:
a strong gale with sleet and snow... which cased everything in ice... our ropes became like wire, our sails like plates of metal.

Captain Cook sailed around Antarctica in 1772–73. He discovered some of the islands, but he couldn't get to the mainland.

Hunters came to Antarctica looking for seals. They didn't tell people where they went because they didn't want anyone else to find the seals. Seal hunters from the United States and the United Kingdom saw, and may have landed on, mainland Antarctica in the 1820s.

James Clark Ross found a way through the pack ice to the mainland. Other explorers followed him.

In 1910–11, two different groups tried to be the first people to get to the South Pole. One group from Norway, led by Roald Amundsen, won. The other group from the United Kingdom, led by R. F. Scott, died on the way back.

Amundsen had spent a long time in Arctic weather practicing for his journey. His group learned how to control dogsleds, and could ski very well. Scott and his group, on the other hand, were poorly prepared. They took ponies, which got stuck in the snow. They had to pull their sleds themselves because they couldn't make the dogs work. Scott's group became slower and more exhausted.

It's easier for us now. When I first came here we still used dogs to get around. Now we use skidoos (say "ski-DOOs") and tractors and aircraft.

The Continent

Antarctica lies under a huge **ice sheet**. The ice sheet is so thick that it makes Antarctica the highest continent in the world. This height is one of the reasons why Antarctica is the coldest place in the world.

The ice is so heavy that a lot of the land has been pushed below sea level.

Cross section of the Antarctic continent

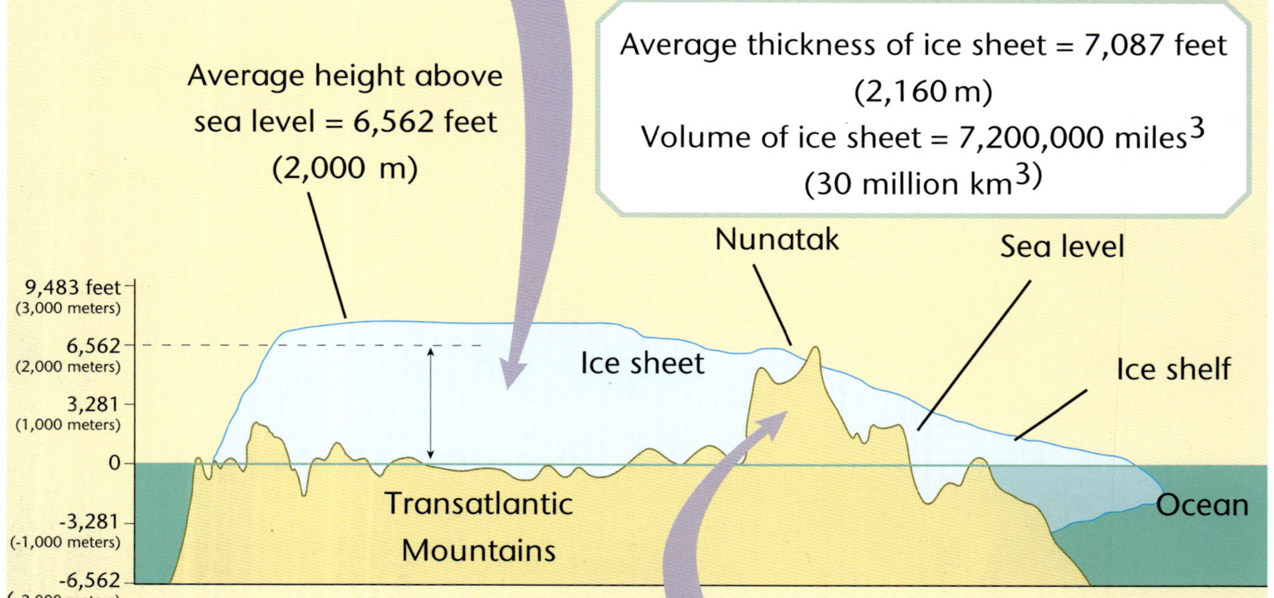

Mountains sticking up out of the ice are called **nunataks**.

 Antarctica:

is 98% covered by an ice sheet.

has a lowest recorded temperature of –128.6ºF (–89.2ºC).

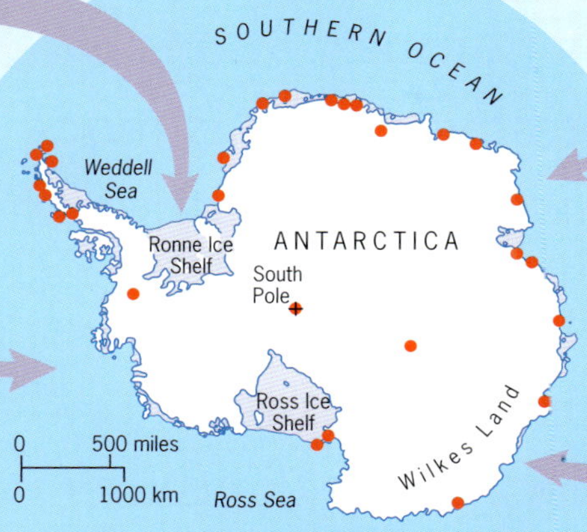

is the fifth largest continent – it is more than 540,553 miles^2 (14 million km^2).

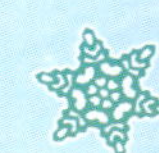

has no people that live there permanently.

People come to study Antarctica and its wildlife. They stay at places called **research stations**. In the summer, there are about 3,000 people in Antarctica. In the winter, most of them go home, and then there are only about 600 people there.

Most places to study in Antarctica are near the coast. Here the temperature is not quite as cold. You can work in the cold until the temperature drops below about -40° F (-40° C). When it gets to -76° F (-60° C), you really need to be inside.

Ice

Freshwater is not salty and is water that you can drink. Freshwater ice is made from freshwater, usually from rain or snow.

Antarctica's ice sheet holds 90 percent of the world's freshwater (as ice and snow). Fewer than 2 inches (5 cm) of snow falls in the center of the ice sheet. It is a cold "desert." Over millions of years, the ice has in some places built up to 2.92 miles (4.7 km) thick.

If the ice sheet melted, the sea level over the Earth would rise by 230 feet (70 m)!

Ice Shelves

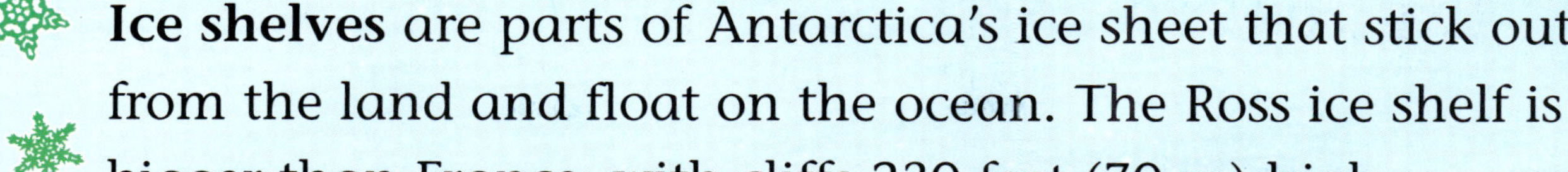

Ice shelves are parts of Antarctica's ice sheet that stick out from the land and float on the ocean. The Ross ice shelf is bigger than France, with cliffs 230 feet (70 m) high.

Icebergs

Icebergs are pieces of the ice shelf that break off in the summer and float off to sea.

Icebergs are made of freshwater ice and snow.

Sea ice forming

Sea ice

Sea ice is made from frozen seawater.

The salt from the sea makes the ice soft.

Sea ice is easier for an icebreaker to break than freshwater ice.

Volcanoes

Mt. Erebus is almost always steaming. There is less snow on its sides than on other nunataks. In the winter, you can sometimes see a red glow from the crater.

Mt. Erebus is on Ross Island. It often puffs out steam. When explorer James Ross first saw it, in 1840, it was spitting fire. The island was named after its discoverer and the volcano after one of Ross's ships.

Even though it is so cold, there are lots of volcanoes in Antarctica. Two are still active.

Deception Island

This island is the top of an underwater volcano. You can sail int[illegible] the crater and get out on the beach. Hot springs on the beaches make them steam every day. It's warm enough to swim in!

Life

Grass

There are hardly any plants on Antarctica.

The biggest animals that live year-round on the land are little flies with no wings.

There are not many places where plants can grow. There are only two flowering plants on Antarctica – a grass and an herb. Otherwise, only mosses and lichens, liverworts, and mushrooms can grow there.

Wingless Antarctic fly

Antarctica is very important for ocean animals. The waters around Antarctica are feeding grounds for all kinds of animals. In the summer, the waters are full of food.

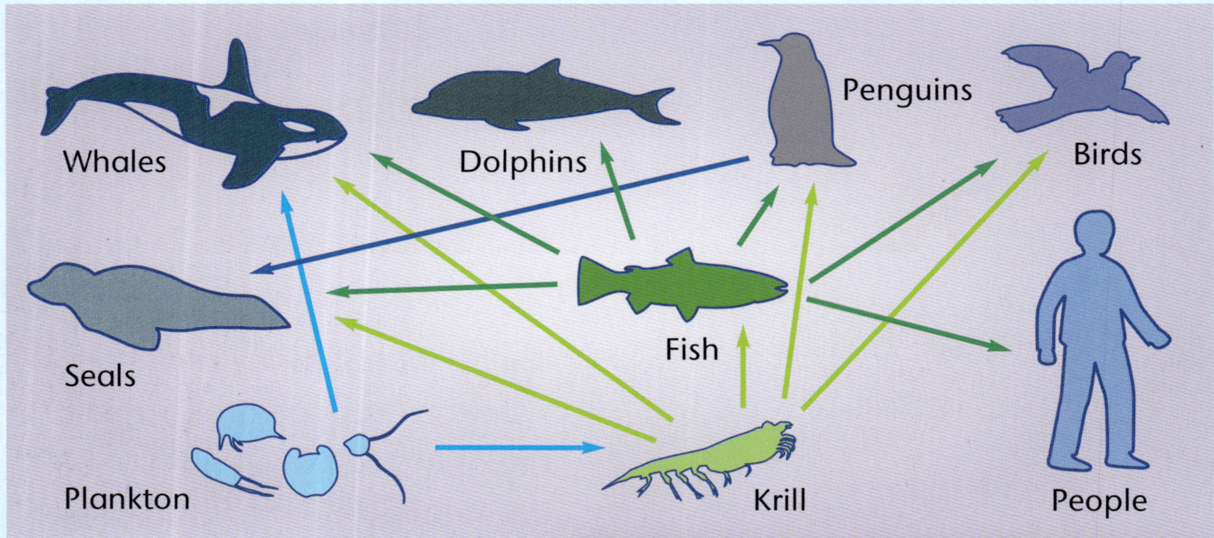

Food web of the southern ocean

Plankton

Many Antarctic animals eat **plankton**.

Close-up: plankton

DEFINITIONS

krill: small shellfish, a little like shrimp. These gather in huge groups of millions and millions

plankton: t
and anim
drift near
of the oce

Krill

Krill are tiny, but whales, seals, penguins, and fish love to eat them.

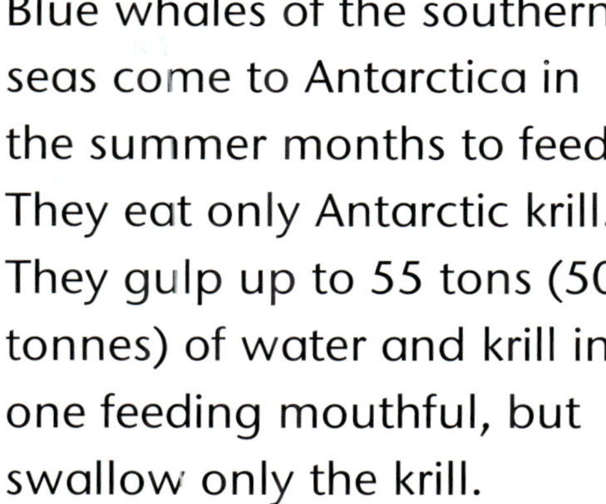

Blue whales of the southern seas come to Antarctica in the summer months to feed. They eat only Antarctic krill. They gulp up to 55 tons (50 tonnes) of water and krill in one feeding mouthful, but swallow only the krill.

Millions of seals and whales have been hunted in Antarctic waters. Today, anglers from many nations are taking squid, krill, and fish. People are trying to stop this overfishing, but there are a lot of poachers.

Penguins

Adelie penguins

A variety of penguins live around Antarctica.

And I've been pecked by all of them! Penguins are very curious and will come right up to you. If you grab one, to measure or tag it, it will peck very hard, and give you karate chops with its flippers!

Macaroni penguin

Penguins don't fly. Their flipper-wings make them the world's greatest swimming and diving birds.

Emperor penguins

In the spring, some of the smaller penguins come ashore and nest on the rocky coast of Antarctica.

They spend the winter out at sea because it is warmer than near the land.

Chinstrap penguins

Gentoo penguins

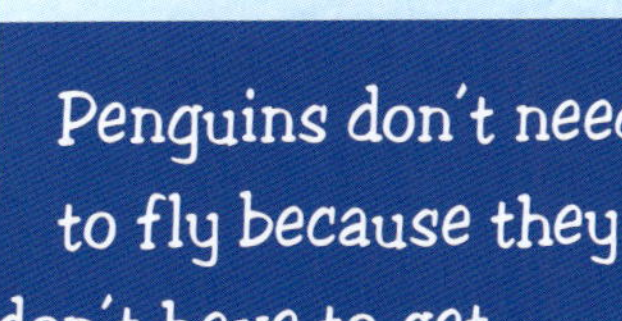

Penguins don't need to fly because they don't have to get away from any land animals – there aren't any! They have to swim well though, to get away from seals.

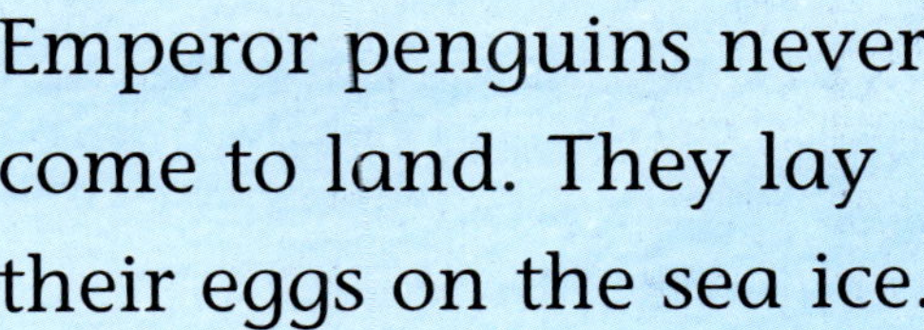

Emperor penguins never come to land. They lay their eggs on the sea ice.

Emperors are the largest penguins, and can weigh up to 100 pounds (45 kg)!

Seals

Weddell seals live only in Antarctica. They can stay underwater for ninety minutes and dive to 1,640 feet (500 m). They are meat eaters.

Weddell seal

Leopard seal

Leopard seals wait under the edge of the ice for penguins to jump in.

Cold Fish

Notothenioid fish

The body temperature of fish in Antarctic waters is below 32ºF (0ºC). To keep their blood from freezing, they have "antifreeze" in their blood.

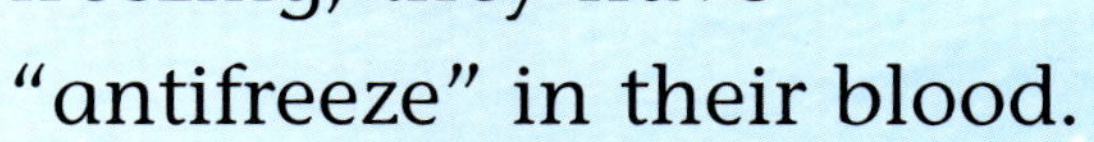

These toothfish grow slowly. They reach more than 6.5 feet (2 m) in length. They live for up to fifty years and don't breed until they are ten.

Patagonian toothfish

Toothfish are supposed to be protected by law, but they are hunted illegally. Anglers use fishing lines that are 12 miles (20 km) long and have hooks all along them.

Dead albatross

Thousands of albatross and other birds are killed every year by illegal fishing. The birds get caught by hooks and drown.

Research

Antarctica is a good place to study weather. The atmosphere is very clear and unpolluted. The weather in Antarctica affects the weather all around the world.

Weather balloon

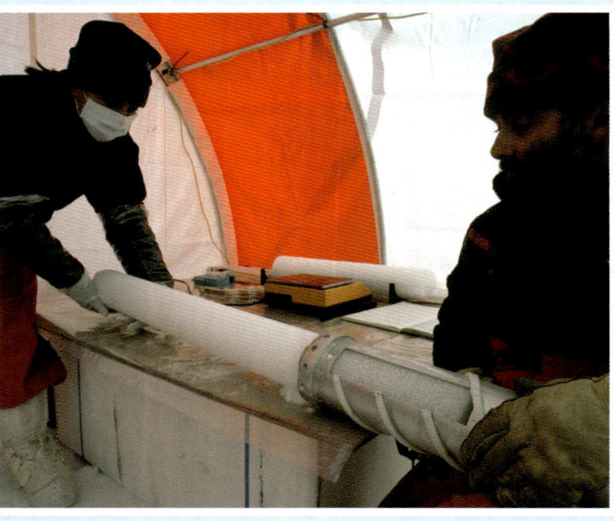

The different layers of this **ice core** show the snow that fell in different years.

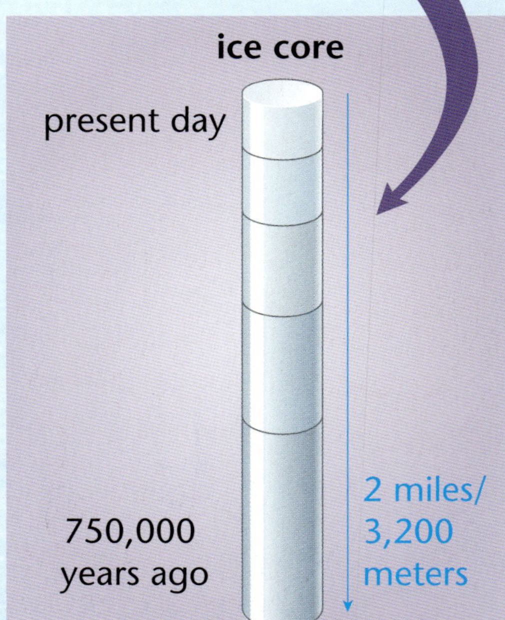

By looking at ice from the ice sheet, people can figure out what the weather was like thousands of years ago.

Fern fossil in Antarctic rock

By looking at the rocks, people have discovered that Antarctica was not always so cold.

You can visit Antarctica as a tourist. Visits take one or two weeks. You'll need to be very careful not to frighten the animals or leave any litter.

Icebreakers

Icebreakers are ships that can sail through icy waters. They ride up onto the ice and use the weight of the ship to break the floe. They can easily get through ice that is 10 feet (3 m) thick.

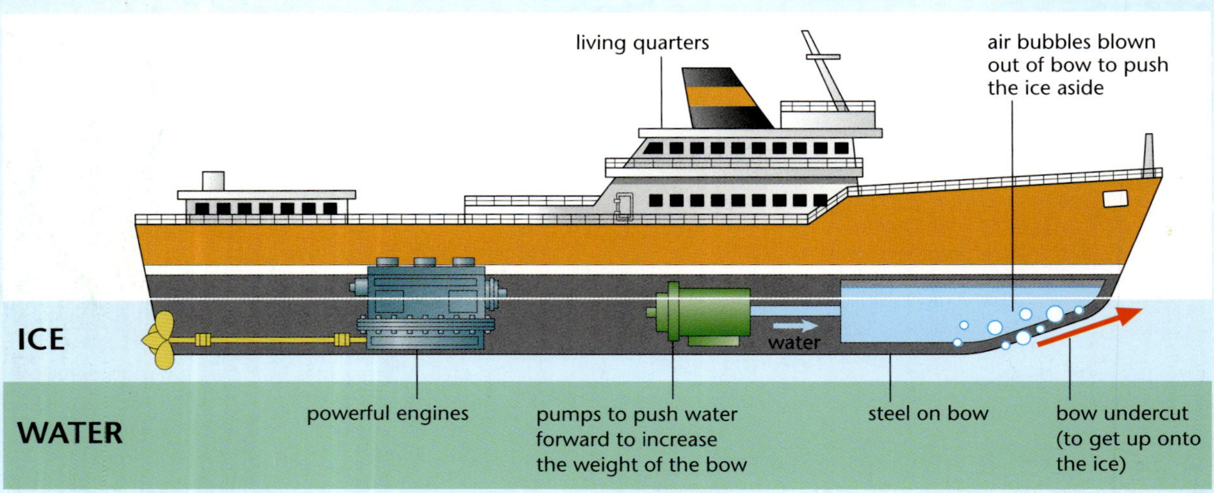

When icebreakers are breaking through thicker, older ice, the ship is very noisy and uncomfortable. People live and sleep near the top of the ship so they don't hear as much noise.

Icebreakers are there to get you out of trouble! When you go into pack ice you try and avoid the ice - you push it around. You only break the ice if you get stuck.

Look Back

1. What food do blue whales eat?
2. Who was the first person to reach the South Pole?
3. What is freshwater ice made of?
4. Which kind of penguin lives its whole life out at sea, or on sea ice?
5. How much of Antarctica is covered in an ice sheet?

Index

Glossary

continent – one of the seven very large land areas in the world

floe – a block of pack ice

ice core – a tube of ice removed from an ice sheet

ice sheet – a wide area of ice

ice shelf – part of an ice sheet that sticks out above, and floats on, the ocean

mainland – the main part of a continent or country. Antarctica has a large mainland with many smaller islands around it.

nunatak – an Antarctic mountain that sticks out of the ice sheet

pack ice – ice that has formed a sheet on the ocean, and then been broken into floes by the swell of the waters

pole – the farthest point south or north in the world

research stations – places where scientists go to stay and study

sea level – the height of the top of the oceans